THEN & NOW

PORTLAND

Opposite: This 1950 view of Monument Square is looking west on Congress Street with Portland's first two skyscrapers, the Fidelity Building of 1910 and the Chapman Building of 1924 shown on the right, with Preble Street coming up between them. Portland's population reached it peak in 1950 when it grew to 77,000 due largely to the more than 30,000 jobs created in the shipyards during World War II, so in many ways, this image captures Portland at its zenith. Today, the population has stabilized at around 65,000. In 1881, historian Edward Elwell had the following to say about this part of the city: "Market [now Monument] Square is to Portland what the Forum was to the ancient Roman cities: a center of business, the scene of popular gatherings, surrounded with stores, hotels, public halls, and places of amusement. We know of no other city where, from the very center of its business streets, one may look out upon such beautiful views of land and water as may be seen from the heart of our city. Stand, at the hour of sunset, at the head of Preble Street, and look out over the waters of Back Cove, reflecting the hues of the sunset sky; upon the green fields and tree-crowned summits of Deering, and tell us if anything can be finer." The same sentiment applies today. (Courtesy of the Maine Historical Society.)

THEN & NOW

PORTLAND

John Moon

*For Margaret Rice (1932–2004), who taught me to walk
with kings but never lose the common touch. To Sarah and Amanda
Rice: travel the world, but remember that Portland will always be your
home. To Philippa: the first of many; Larry King awaits.*

Published by Arcadia Publishing
Charleston SC, Chicago IL, Portsmouth NH, San Francisco CA

Printed in the United States of America

For all general information contact Arcadia Publishing at:
Telephone 843-853-2070
Fax 843-853-0044
E-mail sales@arcadiapublishing.com
For customer service and orders:
Toll-Free 1-888-313-2665

Visit us on the Internet at www.arcadiapublishing.com

On the front cover: With two railroad stations at opposite ends of the city, Portlanders
needed a way to connect them, and thus, in 1850, they filled in the waterfront along
Fore Street to create the aptly named Commercial Street, at 5,993 feet in length and
100 feet in width, with 26 feet in the center reserved for railway purposes. The U.S.
Custom House (pictured) was completed in 1872 at a cost of $485,000 and was designed
by Alfred B. Mullett of the U.S. Department of the Treasury. The horse-drawn wagons
in this image from about 1890 are carrying fish in the barrels, including haddock, cod,
and mackerel, destined for export to a hungry world. (Courtesy of the Maine Historic
Preservation Commission.)

On the back cover: The view is looking northeast from the cupola of the Portland
Observatory on the top of Munjoy Hill, with the islands of Casco Bay in the distance.
Adjoining the observatory stands the Congress Street Methodist Episcopal Church,
erected in 1868. Its summit was the highest object in the city, easily seen from the harbor
and from the sea. Demolished in the 1970s, a fire station now occupies the spot, but the
observatory still stands. (Courtesy of the Maine Historic Preservation Commission.)

Contents

ACKNOWLEDGMENTS

My thanks to everyone who assisted with the research and writing of this book.

I am particularly indebted to Earle G. Shettleworth Jr. and his staff at the Maine Historic Preservation Commission for supplying so many of the vintage images that make this book special. Thanks also to him for reading the manuscript and sharing with me his encyclopedic knowledge of Portland. The citizens of Maine are truly fortunate to have him as a resource.

For their help in a variety of other ways, I wish to thank the following individuals and organizations: Toby Crockett, Greater Portland Landmarks; Kathy DiPhilippo, South Portland Historical Society; Falmouth Historical Society; Freeport Historical Society; Meagan Gaudin, Casey Ryder, Randall Chasse, and Tom Manning, Miss Portland Diner; Peter E. Gribbin, Portland High School; Jim Iacono, Maine Aviation; Lorie Julian, Pierce Promotions; Peter Lekousi, son of James Lekousi; Luminosea Productions; Maine Medical Center; Catherine Michaels; Michael Morrison, digital-illuminations.com; Bill Needleman, City of Portland; Rosemary Orbis, Orbis Mapping Solutions; David Paul, Committee to Restore the Abyssinian Meeting House; Jeff Perkins and Louis Torrier, Amato's; Brian Peterson, Peterson Photography; Ruth Porter, L.L. Bean; John and Judith Rastl; Anne Reagan, the Inn at St. John; Howard C. Reiche Jr.; James and Jennifer Rice; Dale Rines, Walnut Crest Farm; Donald M. Russell Jr.; Daniel Savage; Abraham Schechter, curator of special collections, Portland Public Library; Yolanda Theunissen, Osher Map Library, University of Southern Maine; Thomas Memorial Library, City of Cape Elizabeth; Sherrin Vail, Avesta Housing; Westbrook Historical Society; Leann Wiley, Portland Museum of Art; and last but certainly not least, Bill Barry and Dani Fazio, Maine Historical Society.

Books that I found useful in doing the research for *Portland* include the following: William Willis, *The History of Portland* (1865); Augustus F. Moulton, *Portland by the Sea* (1926); Edward H. Elwell, *Portland and Vicinity* (1881); Greater Portland Landmarks, *Portland* (1972); William Goold, *Portland in the Past* (1886); William David Barry and Francis W. Peabody, *Tate House, Crown of the Mast Trade* (1982); Earle G. Shettleworth Jr. and William David Barry, *Mr. Goodhue Remembers Portland, Scenes from the Mid-19th Century* (1981); Peter E. Gribbin, *A History of Portland High School, 1821 through 1981* (1982); Kenneth E. Thompson Jr., *Portland Head Light & Fort Williams* (1998); Howard C. Reiche Jr., *Closeness, Memories of Mrs. Munjoy's Hill* (2002); and Joyce K. Bibber and Earle G. Shettleworth Jr., *Portland* (2007).

For her encouragement and enthusiasm for this project, I wish to thank my editor at Arcadia Publishing, Hilary Zusman. A special and heartfelt thanks is due to Norman Morse for his generous support in making this book possible.

Unless otherwise noted, all contemporary images in this book are from the author's collection.

INTRODUCTION

Why do we long to preserve?

What is it about an old photograph of a building, a street, or a neighborhood that makes us prickle with recognition, even when the passage of time makes the scene barely discernible today? Why do such images resonate with the reader, staying in our hearts and our minds long after we have closed the book and placed it back on the shelf? Is it merely the nostalgic yearning for another era, a desire to revisit a simpler time, or is there something more fundamental going on? Could it be that we see in these images a glimpse of ourselves? Perhaps they help us to realize on some level that our own individuality, which we so revere, is not entirely our own, and that who we are now is in fact who we were then. In other words, our heritage is important to us.

Architecturally, the Portland of today is predominantly a 19th-century city, built in the days of its greatest prosperity as a seaport and railroad center. But vast areas of the city have been altered and entire blocks simply leveled to the ground. Two events in particular have left a deep and lasting wound in the architectural consciousness of the city. The first was the demolition of the Portland Union Station, torn down in 1961 when rail passenger service ended and replaced with a strip mall. The second was the leveling of the old post office on Middle Street, used first as a parking lot and now as a public park.

When New York's magnificent Pennsylvania station was demolished in 1963, it prompted the renowned Yale architectural historian Vincent Scully to lament, "Once we entered the city like a god; one scuttles in now like a rat." The furor over the demolition of such a well-known landmark is often cited as a catalyst for the architectural preservation movement in the United States. This is true in Portland, where the loss of Portland Union Station and the post office led to the formation of Greater Portland Landmarks to help protect the city's architectural heritage (see page 73 for an early success story). The sense that something irreplaceable had been lost has only strengthened interest in historic preservation.

For the first time, *Portland* brings together vintage photographs and contemporary images, providing a new awareness that, while much has been lost, much also remains. It may be too late to save Portland Union Station, but it is not too late to save the rest of the city. Armed with this knowledge, let us work together to find new ways to maintain the character, quality, and continuity of this beautiful city by the sea.

John Moon
Falmouth
February 2009

ANCIENT
FALMOUTH,
FROM 1630 TO 1690.
For Willis History of Portland.
Bailey & Noyes, Portland, Me.

Present-day Portland was known as Falmouth in precolonial times, a name derived from the ancient Cornwall town at the mouth of the Fal River in England, whence came several early English settlers. As shown on this map, the area included the present-day towns of Portland, South Portland, Cape Elizabeth, Westbrook, and Falmouth. In 1658, under Massachusetts authority, a commission declared, "Those places formerly called Spurwink and Casco Bay, from the east side of the Spurwink River to the Clapboard islands in Casco Bay, shall run back eight miles into the country, and henceforth shall be called Falmouth." It was not until 1786 that Falmouth Neck finally separated from the rest of Falmouth, incorporated as a town, and, with much discussion, was given the name of Portland, after nearby geographical features like Portland Head, Portland Sound, and Portland (now Cushing) Island. The map shows early settlers by name and where they lived between 1630 and 1690, an era characterized by, as historian William David Barry put it, "grinding poverty, guerrilla warfare, and unending litigation." (Courtesy of Michael Morrison, Digital-Illuminations.com.)

DOWNTOWN
AND BAYSIDE

This 1879 view of Market Square shows Portland's old market house, which was constructed in 1825 but modified in 1832 into Portland's first city hall by Charles Quincy Clapp. The old city hall was torn down in 1888 to make room for the Soldiers and Sailors Monument of 1891, which stands at the center of Monument Square today. (Courtesy of the Maine Historic Preservation Commission.)

In this view of Congress Square from about 1885, the white building is the beautiful Matthew Cobb Mansion of 1801, designed by the architect Alexander Parris. Describing its appearance, historian William Goold noted, "its unsullied white front, with no sign of joint or seam, gave it the appearance of being cut from an immense block of white marble, leaving the carved ornaments standing out in relief." Since 1980, it has been the site of the Portland Museum of Art. (Courtesy of the Maine Historical Society.)

This view captures the H. J. Libby home at the northwest corner of High Street and Congress Street around 1925. The Italianate double house of 1852–1853 was designed by Charles A. Alexander and was known for its elaborately painted wall decorations. It was demolished in 1929 to make way for the State building, shown today. The State building provides retail and office space and contains the State Theater, the last of the pre-World War II cinemas left in downtown Portland. (Courtesy of the Maine Historical Society.)

By 1920, the automobile was becoming more predominant than the horse, both of which can be seen in this photograph of Congress Square. The Congress Square Hotel is still there on the left in the contemporary image, and Hay's Drug Store is still seen in the center heater formed where Free Street and Congress Street meet, though today it is occupied by Starbuck's Coffee. The third-story addition was designed by the Stevens firm in 1922. (Courtesy of the Maine Historic Preservation Commission.)

DOWNTOWN AND BAYSIDE

The City Hotel, at the corner of Congress Street and Forest Avenue, was a fashionable place to stay, along with the Preble House and United States Hotel on Monument Square and the Falmouth Hotel on Middle Street. It was torn down in 1894 by Joseph Rines to make way for his new Congress Square Hotel, shown as it looks today. Note that the building to the far left is still there, a relic from a bygone era. (Courtesy of the Maine Historical Society.)

There were many hotels in Portland that catered to the increasing visitor population at the beginning of the 20th century. The Preble House, seen here located next to the Longfellow House, was considered attractive lodging. Commodore Edward Preble originally built his home here between 1806 and 1808 but died before it was completed. It was later turned into the Preble House Hotel but was torn down in 1924 to make way for the Chapman building. (Courtesy of the Maine Historic Preservation Commission.)

This view of Monument Square around 1900 shows the Soldiers and Sailors Monument of 1891 but not Portland's first skyscraper, the Fidelity Bank and Trust, built in 1909–1910. The times were changing. An electric trolley is making its way up Congress Street, and horse-drawn carriages can still be seen moving people across town. In the contemporary image, the Fidelity building and the 1924 Chapman building can both be seen, along with the now pedestrian-friendly square. (Courtesy of the Maine Historic Preservation Commission.)

The white building with the granite facade is the W. T. Kilborn Company on lower Free Street, shown around 1890. Wiped out by the 1866 fire, Kilborn built the four-story structure seen here in 1868 at 24 Free Street, with its handsome front of ornamental design. The front doors were imported from Paris and featured exquisite curved glass, long since replaced. This entire block on lower Free Street is still intact. (Courtesy of the Maine Historical Society.)

This wintertime view of lower Free Street is also from around 1890 but looks up Free Street from the other direction. On the right is the H. H. Hay drugstore at the lower end of Free Street where Middle Street comes in to form a heater. A fourth story was added to the drugstore building in 1919 from designs by John Calvin Stevens. In the contemporary image, one can see all the way up Free Street to Congress Square. (Courtesy of the Maine Historic Preservation Commission.)

The brainchild of Henry Rines, the 12-story Eastland Hotel was heralded as "the most important building project that has ever been carried out in this city" when it opened its doors on June 15, 1927. On June 16, 1927, well-know national radio announcer Graham McNamee dropped a set of hotel keys into Portland harbor with the promise that the Eastland's doors would always stay open. So far, so good. (Courtesy of the Maine Historic Preservation Commission.)

This view of Monument Square was taken from the 10th floor of the 1909–1910 Fidelity building. The building on the lower left corner is the Edwards and Walker hardware store, still remembered by many old-time Portlanders as the place to get nearly anything. It has since been replaced by a modern high-rise office building. In the contemporary image, the glass facade of One City Center is on the left, replacing an entire block once known as the golden triangle. (Courtesy of the Maine Historic Preservation Commission.)

With roots going back to 1821, Portland High School is the second-oldest high school in the nation, preceded only by Boston's English Classical High School, which was founded earlier the same year. The school on Cumberland Avenue was built in 1863 but redesigned in 1918 into a vastly larger E-shaped building with 70 classrooms for 1,300 pupils. Today enrollment is around 1,000, and 25 percent of the students are from over 49 other nations. (Courtesy of the Maine Historic Preservation Commission.)

The original Miss Portland diner opened on March 7, 1949. Over the years, it changed ownership several times and was moved to a spot on Marginal Way, where it was operated for 25 years by Randall Chasse. Upon his retirement in 2004, Chasse donated it to the City of Portland, which moved it again. It has now been restored and enlarged under the caring, new ownership of Portland native Tom Manning and his wife, Stephanie. (Courtesy of Randall Chasse and Miss Portland diner.)

GRAND OPENING
Monday, March 7th At 11 A. M.
'Miss Portland Diner'

24 HOUR SERVICE

AMPLE PARKING FACILITIES

Maine's Largest and Most Modern Streamlined Diner At 175 Forest Ave. Just Below Post Office

Construction by Worcester Lunch Car Co., Builders of the Finest Diners for 43 Years

OPENING DAY SPECIALS

BAKED VIRGINIA HAM Wine Sauce Potato and Vegetables	ROAST VERMONT TOM TURKEY Potato and Vegetables	FRIED CLAMS IN CRUMBS Cole Slaw French Fries
65c	75c	60c
Old Fashioned New England BEEF STEW With Crackers and Pickles	MISS PORTLAND SPECIAL BAR B-Q BEEF Vegetable and Potatoes	INDIVIDUAL CHICKEN PIES Vegetable and Potatoes
45c	65c	60c

MISS PORTLAND DINER

This view is looking north over Back Bay from the bell tower of city hall around 1895. Much change has taken place in the Bayside area over the past 100 years. Large areas of Back Bay have been filled in to accommodate a growing city. In the contemporary view is the new Intermed building on Marginal Way, along with the new student housing structure to its right. (Courtesy of the Maine Historic Preservation Commission.)

This view is looking northeast from the bell tower of city hall around 1895. The Congregational church is on the right with the First Baptist Church behind it. To the left is the Cathedral of the Immaculate Conception, doing well after a recent multiyear renovation. On the horizon atop Munjoy Hill is the 1881 Shailor School, the 1807 Portland Observatory, and lower down the hill is the 1867 North School. (Courtesy of the Maine Historical Society.)

In the 1920s, automobiles were still something of a novelty but coming on strong. Early traffic lights contained as many as seven different colored lenses, leading to confusion and many accidents. To help solve the problem, the Portland Police Department erected signal boxes at key intersections. This one is on Monument Square, with officer George Dennison in the box. The building in the background is the Clapp Block at the corner of Elm and Congress Streets. (Courtesy of the Maine Historical Society.)

CHAPTER 2

MUNJOY HILL AND THE EAST END

George Cleeve settled in Portland in 1632 but sold all his land in 1659 to John Phillips of Boston, whose daughter was married to George Munjoy. Munjoy became a large landowner himself, ultimately owning most of what is now Munjoy Hill, which was named after him. This photograph shows the Portland Observatory atop Munjoy Hill around 1880. (Courtesy of the Maine Historic Preservation Commission.)

The drawing portrays how Munjoy Hill looked in the 1840s. At the top of the hill, Lemuel Moody built his 82-foot-high maritime signal tower in 1807 to alert ship owners of the imminent arrival of their vessels, the last remaining signal tower in the United States. Eastern Cemetery is in the foreground, and Mountfort Street runs left to right down to the waterfront at Fore Street, where George Cleeve and Richard Tucker first settled. (Courtesy of the Maine Historical Society, detail.)

This painting by Charles Codman (1800–1842) portrays Munjoy Hill as it looked in 1829. Notice that there are very few structures on the hill at this time other than the Portland Observatory. It was mostly open pasture used for grazing cattle, training militia, and public recreation. Today the hill is densely packed with two family and three–flatter homes, aptly described by Howard Reiche Jr. as "a whole bunch of people who lived and fit together quite smoothly." (Courtesy of Greater Portland Landmarks.)

The Abyssinian Meeting House was built in 1828 at the foot of Munjoy Hill by Portland's African American community. Closed in 1917, the City of Portland eventually seized the building for unpaid taxes. In 1998, community leaders founded the Committee to Restore the Abyssinian and acquired the building. It is presently engaged in a multiyear restoration effort, which is poised to be of local, state, and national significance. To learn more about the project, visit www.abyme.org. (Courtesy of the Maine Historical Society.)

This vintage image was labeled "unidentified street in Portland." However, the large grain elevator gives it away as the lower end of Mountfort Street, a very old section of Portland. It is at the base of Mountfort Street where George Cleeve and Richard Tucker first settled in 1632 next to a "runnett" of water. With the grain elevators now gone, this gives a glimpse of what they may have seen as they gazed seaward from their home. (Courtesy of the Maine Historic Preservation Commission.)

Portland's Grand Trunk Railway station (1903–1966) serviced the rail route from Portland to Montreal, Canada. It was the brainchild of John A. Poor, who in 1845 drove a horse-drawn sleigh through a blinding snowstorm all the way to Montreal to prove the route. By the 1960s, the Grand Trunk was absorbed into the government-owned Canadian National Railway, and the station was demolished, leaving only the office building at the far right to mark a once-imposing complex. (Courtesy of the Maine Historic Preservation Commission.)

MUNJOY HILL AND THE EAST END

In 1902, a young Italian immigrant named Giovanni Amato began selling fresh-baked rolls filled with meat, cheese, and fresh vegetables to his fellow countrymen working the docks, and the "real Italian sandwich" was born. Amato sold the business in 1972 to Dominic Reali, and today there are 12 company stores and a successful franchise operation. The delicious "real Italian sandwich" is a Portland original. Shown here is the original India Street store. (Courtesy of Amato's.)

"Holy Snow Banks, Batman!" The Munjoy Hill loop of the electric trolley turned right off Congress Street onto Morning Street, down to the Eastern Promenade near Fort Allen Park, right on Atlantic Street, and then back to Congress Street and downtown. This view is from Morning Street looking up toward Congress Street. The trolley's plows made for some incredibly high snow banks, which were great fun for neighborhood children to make snow forts in. (Courtesy of the Maine Historic Preservation Commission.)

This painting by Maine artist Charles Beckett (1814–1866) shows a view looking north from Munjoy Hill around 1850. The view shows Martin's Point, formerly the site of the Marine Hospital, Grand Trunk bridge, and the Veranda Hotel. Today the land shown jutting out into the water is owned by a private medical group, appropriately named Martin's Point Healthcare. (Courtesy of the Maine Historical Society.)

This view shows a man and his two-horsepower carriage, taking a leisurely drive along the Eastern Promenade at the foot of Morning Street. The trolley tracks in the middle of Morning Street can be seen coming down from Congress Street, part of the Munjoy Hill loop, making the turn on the promenade before returning to Congress Street on Atlantic Street. The character of the neighborhood has changed very little over the years, other than the mode of transportation. (Courtesy of the Maine Historic Preservation Commission.)

On the Eastern Promedade, just around the corner from the view on page 36, two men are enjoying a wintertime excursion in a brand new 1907 Knox runabout. Pictured are racecar driver A. L. Dennison with passenger E. H. Cushman of the Portland Company. The Eastern Promenade locale is adjacent to the company's facilities at the foot of Fore Street and was used often as a place to display new automobiles. In 1908, the Portland Company became the exclusive Maine distributor for Knox automobiles. (Courtesy of the Maine Historical Society.)

The bridge spanning the entrance to Portland's Back Bay has always been called Tukey's Bridge. In 1796, private citizens formed a corporation and opened the Back Cove bridge as a toll bridge. Ever since, the popular mind has called it after the bridge's original toll taker, Lemuel Tukey, even though it has been a free bridge since 1837 when a group of Back Cove men threw the tollgate into the sea. (Courtesy of the Maine Historic Preservation Commission.)

The Eastern Cemetery at the foot of Munjoy Hill is Portland's oldest burying ground, dating back to the 17th century. In 1858, the city suspended most burials there. The monuments shown are those of Lt. William Burrows and Capt. Samuel Blythe, killed during the famous battle of Casco Bay in 1813 and buried side by side. The contemporary photograph gives a good perspective of Eastern Cemetery relative to the rest of Portland. (Courtesy of the Maine Historic Preservation Commission.)

At the foot of Congress Street on the Eastern Promenade is the official granite monument erected in 1883 to honor George Cleeve and Richard Tucker, who first settled the Portland peninsula in 1632. A more recent statue of Cleeve, commissioned by his descendants as a gift to the city of Portland, now overlooks the harbor on the property of the Portland Company quite near the original home site. (Courtesy of the Maine Historic Preservation Commission.)

CHAPTER 3

THE OLD PORT
AND WATERFRONT

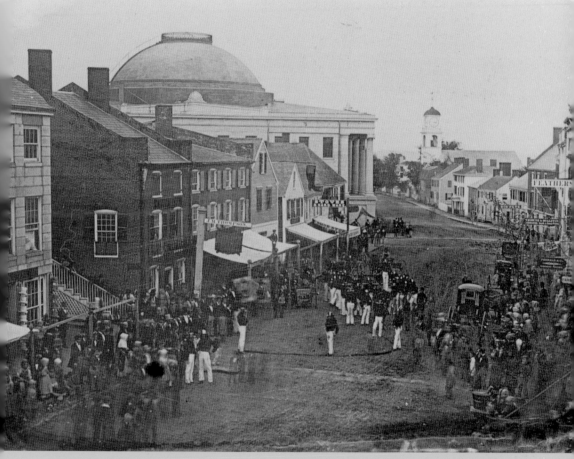

This is Middle Street in 1846 in a rare image of Portland prior to the 1866 fire. The domed building is the Exchange building, constructed between 1836 and 1839 and burned in 1854. It is frequently given as an example of the temple style of Greek Revival architecture that was once an important visual factor in the Portland scene. (Courtesy of the Maine Historic Preservation Commission.)

A man is shown with two oxen and a cart working the streets of Portland around 1890. They are taking a leisurely early morning stroll down Fore Street. On the left are the distinctive second-floor windows of the old Seaman's Club, designed by Charles Quincy Clapp in 1866–1867.

With its four intertwining arches topped by three medallions all circumscribed by a gently rounded arch, this broad expanse of windows anticipates later Victorian commercial facades. (Courtesy of the Maine Historical Society.)

Boothby Square is a small park on Fore Street given to the city in 1902 by Col. Frederick E. Boothby. His gift included a granite water fountain, which was sold at an auction but recently returned to the square after being absent for several years. This view looking east on Fore Street from Market to Pearl Streets includes a row of commercial buildings dating back to 1792. In the contemporary image, the new Evie Cianchette Block is shown on the right. (Courtesy of the Maine Historic Preservation Commission.)

The Mariner's Church was built in 1828–1829 to provide a seaman's chapel for the religious edification of mariners. Its architectural scheme is similar to Faneuil Hall in Boston. Once owned by Asa Clapp, it was sold in 1934 to the C. H. Robinson Company paper firm. It, in turn, sold the building to Frank Akers in 1970. Today it houses several fine shops, including the Fore Street Gallery, where Lorrie Maciag has a fine selection of Paul Black paintings. (Courtesy of Greater Portland Landmarks.)

This State of Maine Armory in the Old Port was built in 1895 for drilling the many National Guard units that were stationed there. The building was designed by Frederick A. Tompson and was later used as a warehouse when its military function ceased. Today it serves as one of the area's more upscale hotels, the Portland Regency. Just two blocks from the waterfront, this is an excellent example of historic preservation that works. (Courtesy of the Maine Historic Preservation Commission.)

First laid out in 1724, Exchange Street was originally called Fish Street, probably because it ran down to the docks when Fore Street was the waterfront. Originally home to several banks, the board of trade, and the merchant's exchange, it later came to be occupied by printers, insurance companies, and stock brokers. Today Exchange Street is the liveliest in the Old Port, lined with retail shops of every description. (Courtesy of the Maine Historic Preservation Commission.)

The post office at Middle and Exchange Streets was constructed between 1868 and 1871 of Vermont marble and designed by U.S. Department of the Treasury architect Alfred B. Mullett. As originally planned, the post office was on the ground floor, and the second story was used for United States court rooms and offices. This magnificent building was torn down in 1965 for a parking lot. Today the area is an open park known as post office square. (Courtesy of the Maine Historic Preservation Commission.)

This unidentified alley from the 1920s is a view of Wharf Street, which runs parallel to Fore Street and probably got its name from the fact that it once ran along the wharfs when Fore Street was the waterfront. That all changed in 1850 when it was decided to fill in a portion of the harbor to create Commercial Street. The contemporary view shows Gritty McDuff's on the left and retail shops on the right. (Courtesy of the Maine Historic Preservation Commission.)

The vintage image shows the south side of Middle Street between Exchange and Union Streets just after the 1866 fire. On the left is the 1867 Boyd Block, designed by George M. Harding, and on the right is John Bundy Brown's Falmouth Hotel, built from 1866 to 1868 and designed by Charles A. Alexander. Only the Boyd Block (with an additional story added on its top) and the building next to it remain. (Courtesy of the Maine Historic Preservation Commission.)

The vintage view is looking west on Middle Street toward the intersection of Union Street. At center left is the Falmouth Hotel, now gone, while at the immediate right is the Oxford Block, built in 1886 and 1887 from designs by John Calvin Stevens, who maintained his architectural office on the top floor. The white-faced building on the right in both images is the old Casco Bank building. (Courtesy of the Maine Historic Preservation Commission.)

This view is standing at Middle and Exchange Streets looking north to the Portland City Hall on Congress Street. The domed city hall burned in 1908, so the vintage image is from earlier than that. At left in the foreground is the one-story wooden Fox Block, now demolished, which held small shops, and the marble post office looms on the right. In the contemporary image, the facade of the building on the left is a painted mural, while on the right is the beautiful Portland Savings Bank. (Courtesy of the Maine Historic Preservation Commission.)

No building better symbolized the rebirth of Portland's commercial district after the 1866 fire than the Falmouth Hotel at Middle and Union Streets. Erected in 1867 and 1868 by John Bundy Brown, the six-story Falmouth featured a grand sandstone facade and contained 240 guest rooms, a dining room, a billiard room, and 10 stores. It was razed in 1963–1964 after nearly a century of service. Today it is the site of the Key Bank Plaza. (Courtesy of the Maine Historic Preservation Commission.)

First organized in 1869, the Portland Yacht Club built this clubhouse on the end of Central Wharf in 1885. It burned in 1926 and was replaced the following year by a lower building, designed by John Calvin Stevens, a yacht club member (see page 92 for Stevens's version). In 1947, the yacht club purchased property in Falmouth Foreside and moved to a new facility there where it has been ever since. (Courtesy of the Maine Historic Preservation Commission.)

Portland likes to pride itself on maintaining a working waterfront, which brings to mind images like the vintage picture shown here. Fishing vessels, mostly sloops and schooners, once crowded around the waterfront docks. While there is still a commercial fishing industry in Portland, for better or for worse, one is more likely to see continued development of the waterfront into condominiums, like those shown here at Chandler's wharf. (Courtesy of the Maine Historic Preservation Commission.)

4

THE WEST END AND DEERING

Capt. George Tate Sr. came to Stroudwater Landing in 1750 as a senior mast agent and in 1755 built one of the finest homes in the Casco Bay region. Today the Tate House is a rare and elegant survivor of the period, standing as Portland's oldest registered national historic landmark. (Courtesy of the Maine Historic Preservation Commission.)

This is the West End Hotel at the corner of Congress and St. John Streets in the 1920s. In the contemporary image, the building with the Greyhound painted on the side is the Pizza Villa Restaurant, which previously was attached to the back side of the hotel but left standing when the hotel was demolished. Today this corner lot is home to the Vermont Trailways bus terminal. A large parking garage of the Maine Medical Center is in the background. (Courtesy of Peter Lekousi.)

THE WEST END AND DEERING

This is Portland Union Station around 1959. It was built in 1888 to serve as Portland's rail terminus from all parts of the northeast. Designed by Bostonians Bradlee, Winslow, and Wetherell, it was constructed to serve both the Boston and Maine and the Maine Central Railroads. It was demolished in 1961, and the eight-acre site was sold to a Boston developer, who built a shopping center there. Its destruction heralded the beginning of Portland's historic preservation movement. (Courtesy of Peter Lekousi.)

Envisioned by Mayor James P. Baxter in the 1890s, a boulevard was constructed around the shore of Back Cove in 1916–1917. Linking Forest Avenue to Washington Avenue, the 2¼ mile roadway helped to open the Deering suburbs to residential development and provided a beautiful drive from which to view the city. (Courtesy of the Maine Historic Preservation Commission.)

Modern Stroudwater is close to the international jetport, which began as a private flying field for two local men before being first leased by the city and, in 1934, taken over as Portland Municipal Airport. The 1940 terminal was later enlarged and still later replaced by a modern facility. The airport itself also grew in size to the extent that the original terminal shown here is almost impossible to find. Today the building is used by Maine Aviation as a flying school but is scheduled for demolition in 2010. (Courtesy of the Maine Historic Preservation Commission.)

At the heart of today's Maine Medical Center complex is the Maine General Hospital, built on Arsenal Street between 1871 and 1892. Designed in the High Victorian Gothic style by Francis H. Fassett, the brick-and-stone building was based on state-of-the-art hospitals in Boston and New York. Portlanders raised $100,000 towards its construction through fairs, sales, and donations. Though not completed until 1892, the modern hospital facility with its lovely view of the White Mountains was accepting patients by 1874, who paid from $7 to $25 weekly. (Courtesy of the Maine Historic Preservation Commission.)

Judge Nathan Clifford of Portland served on the U.S. Supreme Court from 1858 until his death in 1881. The Clifford Elementary School, named after him, stands on Falmouth Street a few blocks from the present University of Southern Maine. It was built in 1906 and designed by architects John Calvin Stevens and John Howard Stevens. Talk of tearing it down has been squashed, and this grand, old building will probably live on as apartments. (Courtesy of the Maine Historic Preservation Commission.)

The heart of the mast trade was at Stroudwater Landing. On the other side of the Fore River, the small, rapid Stroudwater River (shown here) tumbled into the tidal system. On the left are the backyards of homes such as the George Tate House (see page 55), and on the right was the original site of Harrow House, residence of Col. Thomas Westbrook, the area's first mast agent. (Courtesy of the Maine Historic Preservation Commission.)

On August 27, 1727, Col. Thomas Westbrook was named mast agent and admitted as an inhabitant of Falmouth. In this picture just to the left of the waterfall, he built a garrisoned stockade called Harrow House and set up sawmills, gristmills, and paper mills on the Stroudwater River and elsewhere. In later years, the river was damned up to form a canoe club (pictured) as a form of recreation for local residents. (Courtesy of the Maine Historic Preservation Commission.)

The vintage image shows an aerial view of Portland's West End around 1950, with Portland Union Station at the lower left and Maine General Hospital and the Bramhall-Vaughan Street Reservoir at center right. The contemporary image shows a nearly similar scene today. lPortland Union Station was demolished in 1961, and the Maine Medical Center now dominates the entire hill on the Western Promenade and lower Congress Street. (Vintage image, courtesy of the Maine Historical Society; contemporary image, courtesy of the Maine Medical Center.)

The vintage image shows an aerial view of Portland from around 1940 with the Deering Estate at center flanked by Forest Avenue and Bedford Street. The land was purchased by the Portland Junior College in 1946 and is now the site of the University of Southern Maine. The tall building at right is the National Biscuit Company's (Nabisco) bakery facilities, now the university's Glickman Library. (Vintage image, courtesy of the Maine Historical Society; contemporary image, Brian Peterson Photography.)

This wonderful photograph from the 1920s shows a slice of life as it was once lived in Portland, with a small gasoline station on Forest Avenue and some very tall gasoline pumps. The building in the background is recognized as Nabisco's baking facility. Originally the Huston Biscuit Company, the "baker of Better Biscuits since 1869," the company had its new bakery built near the Deering property in 1919–1920. It is now the University of Southern Maine's Glickman Library. (Courtesy of the Maine Historical Society.)

This shows the same corner as it appeared in the 1930s, with Nabisco in the background. After being used by Nabisco and later serving as a warehouse, the building was remodeled to become the Glickman Library of the University of Southern Maine beginning in 1993. (Courtesy of the Maine Historic Preservation Commission.)

This is the United States Marine Hospital, designed by Ammi Young and built in 1859 on Martin's Point beside the mouth of the Presumpscot River (see also page 35). Set in extensive grounds, the facility provided care for ailing merchant sailors, both coastal and deepwater, until their numbers so declined that it was not needed. It now houses a modern health care facility, Martin's Point Healthcare. (Courtesy of the Maine Historic Preservation Commission.)

CHAPTER 5

STREETSCAPES

The diversity of architectural styles that exists in some parts of Portland helps to make the city the pleasant place that it is. Pictured here is the 1860 home of W. T. Kilborn at 204 Brackett Street.

Note how this stately home helps to define the character of the neighborhood. It has since been demolished for a parking lot. (Courtesy of Donald M. Russell Jr.)

The vintage photograph shows a typical scene on Congress Street looking west from Monument Square in 1901. Shoppers mull along the sidewalk, a man hurries to board a passing trolley, and a horse-drawn carriage attempts to cross the street ahead of it. In just a few years, the automobile would come to dominate the scene. In the contemporary view, a bicycle slowly threads its way up Congress Street among the hustle and bustle of the cars. (Courtesy of the Maine Historical Society.)

STREETSCAPES

The vintage image shows a view of Market Square, looking down Congress Street from approximately in front of the Longfellow House around 1888, just before the old city hall was demolished to put up the Soldiers and Sailors Monument. Various commercial ventures can be seen on both sides of the street, including a sale on strawberry shortcake. A sandwich board sign advertises bargains in parasols and tailor-cut corsets. A similar sign can be seen today in the contemporary image. (Courtesy of the Maine Historical Society.)

This is a view of Spring Street as it appeared in the late 1800s. At left are the Ionic columns of the Charles Quincy Clapp residence at 97 Spring Street. As the son of Asa Clapp, he came from an enterprising family and married well. Like his father, he was a land and building speculator and, like Thomas Jefferson, a gentleman architect. Sadly, almost the entire length of Spring Street has been demolished. (Courtesy of the Maine Historic Preservation Commission.)

The stunning John J. Brown house at 86 Spring Street sat just across from the Clapp house. It was designed by architect Henry Rowe and built in 1845. In 1971, the house was saved from certain demolition by Greater Portland Landmarks, which purchased it and moved it to another location at 387 Spring Street. Today the home has been lovingly restored and is enjoyed by its present owners. (Vintage and contemporary images courtesy of Greater Portland Landmarks.)

This is a view of State Street as it appeared in the 19th century. Laid out in 1800 with broad esplanades and a double tow of elm trees, State Street was Portland's most fashionable neighborhood in the first half of the 19th century. The fourth building from the left in this south-looking view is, for now, the present-day home of Greater Portland Landmarks. Next to it is the State Street Church of 1851, designed by William Washburn of Boston and given a brownstone facade by John Calvin Stevens in 1892 and 1893. (Courtesy of the Maine Historic Preservation Commission.)

Here again is State Street, this time looking north towards Longfellow Square from in front of the State Street Church. Here one sees clearly the double row of elms planted in 1800 that are no longer a part of the State Street scene, lost to disease in the 1960s. Across the street on the left is the foreboding front of the 1847 Thomas O'Brion house, which was purchased later on by Albert Rines and survives today as the Conroy Tully Funeral Home. (Courtesy of the Maine Historic Preservation Commission.)

This view is of Congress Street looking east towards Congress Square in the late 1800s. One of Francis H. Fassett's finest designs was his brownstone Romanesque facade for the Portland Public Library, built in 1887–1888, which can be seen on the left side of both photographs. A gift to the city by James P. Baxter, the building served readers for nearly a century before becoming part of the Maine College of Art. (Courtesy of the Maine Historic Preservation Commission.)

High Street was a fashionable address in the late 1800s. This view is looking toward the waterfront from Congress Square. The second building on the right in the vintage image is the home of wealthy merchant and ship owner Stephen McLellan, built by John Kimball Sr., the prolific builder of Federal-style homes from Ipswich, Massachusetts. Since 1895, it has been the home of the Cumberland Club. Also in the vintage image, the trolley tracks are making the turn to go down Congress Street at Congress Square. (Courtesy of the Maine Historical Society.)

In 1800, merchant brothers Hugh and Stephen McLellan built their three-story brick Federal mansions in the emerging Spring Street neighborhood. John Kimball Sr. was paid $20,000 apiece for the design and construction of each. Hugh's house (see page 79) became part of the art museum, while Stephen's (shown here) has been home to the Cumberland Club since 1895. Both brothers were ruined by the War of 1812 when shipping came to a standstill, causing both to go bankrupt. (Courtesy of the Maine Historic Preservation Commission.)

The McLellan-Sweat mansion at Spring and High Streets, designed by Kimball, was built in 1800 for shipping magnate Hugh McClellan, a one-time business partner of Asa Clapp. Clapp purchased the $20,000 home in 1817 for $4,050. Today the McLellan-Sweat mansion is a part of the Portland Museum of Art. (Courtesy of the Maine Historical Society.)

Henry Wadsworth Longfellow was born in this house at Fore and Hancock Streets in 1807, which was then waterfront property. Reflecting the widespread enthusiasm for Longfellow's poetry, the International Longfellow Society acquired the property in 1914 and opened it as a literary shrine. Tastes in poetry changed, later efforts to preserve the house failed, and it was demolished in 1955. The site is now home to a new Marriott Hotel, shown under construction in 2009. (Courtesy of the Maine Historic Preservation Commission.)

The right half of this brick double house was the home of U.S. congressman Thomas Brackett Reed from 1888 until his death in 1902. Born in Portland in 1839, his social circle included intellectuals and politicians from Pres. Theodore Roosevelt to Mark Twain. In this vintage view, Roosevelt (1858–1919) waves his hat to a crowd of well-wishers outside the home of his friend in Portland on August 26, 1902. (Courtesy of the Maine Historical Society.)

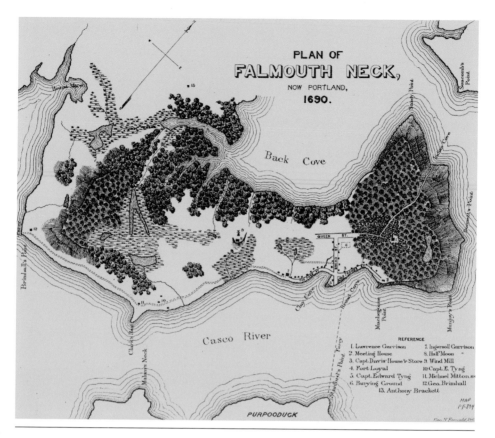

An early map from 1690 shows Portland, then known as Falmouth Neck, as a land dominated by forests and swamps. In the remarkable contemporary image produced by satellite imaging, the full extent of the changes to the peninsula over the past 300 years can be seen. Much land has been filled in, particularly in the Bayside area and along the Portland waterfront when Commercial Street was built in 1850. (Vintage image, courtesy of the Maine Historical Society; contemporary image, courtesy of Orbis Mapping Solutions.)

DAY TRIPS AROUND PORTLAND

While in Portland, it is well worth a short drive to Brunswick to visit Bowdoin College's historically significant Walker Art Museum, recently the beneficiary of a $20 million face-lift. The 1894 landmark museum was designed by Charles Follen McKim of McKim, Mead, and White, who also designed New York's original Pennsylvania station, used from 1910 to 1963. (Courtesy of the Maine Historic Preservation Commission.)

With more than four million visitors a year going to its retail store in Freeport, L.L. Bean looms large in the local economy. Shown here is how the post office square in Freeport looked in 1912, the year the company opened his first store, a tiny shop in the Libby Block on the right. Today the square includes the present L.L. Bean store on the left. (Courtesy of the Maine Historic Preservation Commission.)

By the 1920s, Leon Leonwood Bean moved his store across the street to the second floor of the Warren Block. Rumor has it that a chute connected the second-floor store to the post office below, thus facilitating the early mail-order business. With annual sales now in excess of $1.5 billion, the company's one simple rule seems to have worked: "Sell good merchandise at a reasonable profit, treat your customers like human beings, and they will always come back for more." (Courtesy of L.L. Bean.)

In 1872, an iron tower was erected at Stanford's Point to replace an earlier wooden structure that was built around 1855. It was modeled after the Choregic Monument of Lysicrates and cast by the Portland Company. After the light was automated in 1935, the keeper's house was removed, giving it the appearance it has today. Commonly called Bug Light, it is now part of a spacious new park in South Portland. (Courtesy of the Maine Historic Preservation Commission.)

At the start of World War II, Todd–Bath Iron Shipbuilding Corporation won a contract to build Liberty ships at Cushing Point in South Portland. In this 1943 photograph, the bow of a ship under construction rests on way No. 5 of the west yard. The company ultimately employed over 30,000 men and women and produced 266 Liberty ships. To commemorate their achievement, the replica Liberty ship shown is proudly displayed today in Bug Light Park. (Courtesy of the Maine Historical Society.)

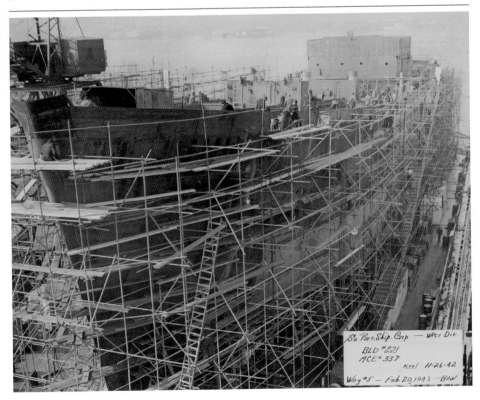

Spring Point Light was built on an underwater ledge off Fort Preble in 1896–1897. For more than 50 years, it stood surrounded by water. In 1950, a breakwater was built connecting it to the South Portland mainland. It is now a favorite destination for residents and tourists alike who can walk along the rocks and explore the lighthouse. On the day this particular photograph was taken, Portland had a royal visitor, the *Queen Mary II.* (Courtesy of the Maine Historic Preservation Commission.)

Overlooking the peaceful Riverside Cemetery and the Spurwink marsh, the Spurwink Meetinghouse has stood its ground in Cape Elizabeth since 1802 as the oldest meetinghouse in town. With its blend of Federal, Gothic, and Greek Revival styles, it is a simple structure with a sparse Puritan décor. Closed since 1957 for regular services but still open by reservation for weddings, funerals, and christenings, it is now owned by the town of Cape Elizabeth. (Courtesy of the Maine Historic Preservation Commission.)

The 1858 Goddard Mansion was the home of Col. John Goddard and his family, designed by Charles A. Alexander. In 1900, it was acquired by the federal government, which eventually converted it to quarters for noncommissioned officers. By March 1981, the decision was made to burn the interior of the structure to remove dangerous debris. Today the proud old mansion stands as a stately ruin, part of Fort Williams Park in Cape Elizabeth. (Courtesy of the Thomas Memorial Library.)

Symbolizing the rockbound coast of Maine, the lighthouse at Portland Head, officially designated Portland Head Light, has aided mariners for over 200 years. Begun by the Massachusetts legislature in 1787, the United States Congress authorized additional expenditures in 1790 to complete the project, and the tower was first lighted on January 10, 1791, with 16 lamps of whale oil. Today Portland Head Light is widely recognized as the most photographed lighthouse in the world. (Courtesy of the Maine Historic Preservation Commission.)

The Portland Yacht Club built its first clubhouse on the end of Central Wharf in Portland in 1885, but that structure burned in 1926 and was replaced the following year by a lower building (pictured), designed by yacht club member John Calvin Stevens.

In 1946, the club purchased a private estate in Falmouth Foreside (pictured) and announced its intention to move there in 1947, where it has been located ever since. (Courtesy of the Portland Yacht Club.)

The faded photograph taken in 1922 portrays what was then Gibson's Ice Cream parlor and gasoline station, located along the old Boston Post Road (Route 88) in Falmouth. Today the Town Landing Market in Falmouth is a local landmark, famous for its "fresh native ice cubes" and the best lobster roll to be had in the entire state of Maine. The store has been owned since 1981 by Dan Groves and his wife. (Courtesy of Falmouth Town Landing Market.)

Bramhall was the private estate of Portland sugar baron John Bundy Brown, built between 1855 and 1858 on the Western Promenade from a design by Charles A. Alexander. The estate was demolished in 1915, but the entrance gate (made by the Portland Company) and granite columns have been preserved. They now grace the entrance to Thornhurst Road in Falmouth, as seen by the letter *B* in the center of the gate. (Courtesy of the Maine Historic Preservation Commission.)

Joseph Rines purchased the former James Phinney Baxter mansion and property in Gorham just over the Westbrook line in 1894. Walnut Crest Farm supplied most of the dairy products for the Columbia, Congress Square, and Eastland Hotels in Portland and for the Danish Village in Scarborough, all properties of the Rines brothers. Rines's grandson Bernard Rines and his sons Dale, Mathew, and Stephen run the farm today, still in the family after all these years. The mansion has been demolished. (Courtesy of Walnut Crest Farm.)

ACROSS AMERICA, PEOPLE ARE DISCOVERING SOMETHING WONDERFUL. *THEIR HERITAGE.*

Arcadia Publishing is the leading local history publisher in the United States. With more than 3,000 titles in print and hundreds of new titles released every year, Arcadia has extensive specialized experience chronicling the history of communities and celebrating America's hidden stories, bringing to life the people, places, and events from the past. To discover the history of other communities across the nation, please visit:

www.arcadiapublishing.com

Customized search tools allow you to find regional history books about the town where you grew up, the cities where your friends and family live, the town where your parents met, or even that retirement spot you've been dreaming about.